KT-872-596

Real Life

GUIDES

CATERING

WITHDRAWN

0 8 SEP 2009

REAL LIFE GUIDES

Practical guides for practical people

In this increasingly sophisticated world the need for manually skilled people to build our homes, cut our hair, fix our boilers and make our cars go is greater than ever. As things progress, so the level of training and competence required of our skilled manual workers increases. In this series of career guides from Trotman, we look in detail at what it takes to train for, get into and be successful at a wide spectrum of practical careers. *Real Life Guides* aim to inform and inspire young people and adults alike by providing comprehensive yet hard-hitting and often blunt information about what it takes to succeed in these areas.

The other titles in the series are:

Real Life Guide: The Armed Forces
Real Life Guide: The Beauty Industry
Real Life Guide: Care
Real Life Guide: Carpentry and Cabinet-Making
Real Life Guide: Catering
Real Life Guide: Construction
Real Life Guide: Distribution and Logistics
Real Life Guide: Electrician
Real Life Guide: The Fire Service
Real Life Guide: Hairdressing
Real Life Guide: Plumbing
Real Life Guide: The Police Force
Real Life Guide: Retailing
Real Life Guide: Transport
Real Life Guide: Working Outdoors
Real Life Guide: Working with Animals and Wildlife
Real Life Guide: Working with Young People

trotman

Real Life GUIDES

CATERING

Dee Pilgrim

Second edition

Real Life Guide to Catering
This second edition published in 2007 by Trotman
an imprint of Crimson Publishing,
Westminster House, Kew Road, Richmond, Surrey TW9 2ND
www.crimsonpublishing.co.uk
Reprinted 2008
© Trotman 2007, 2003
First edition published 2003 by Trotman and Co Ltd

Editorial and Publishing Team
Author Dee Pilgrim
Editorial Mina Patria, Publishing Director; Jessica Spencer,
Development Editor; Jo Jacomb, Editorial Manager; Ian Turner,
Production Editor
Production John O'Toole, Operations Manager
Marketing Catherine Slinn, Marketing Executive
Advertising Sarah Talbot, Advertising Sales Director

Designed by XAB

British Library Cataloguing in Publications Data
A catalogue record for this book is available from the British
Library

ISBN 978 1 84455 136 1

Typeset by Mac Style, Nafferton, East Yorkshire
Printed and bound in Great Britain by Bell & Bain Ltd, Glasgow

Real Life GUIDES

CONTENTS

About the author

Dee Pilgrim completed the pre-entry, periodical journalism course at the London College of Printing before working on a variety of music and women's titles. She has written numerous articles and interviews for *Company, Cosmopolitan, New Woman, Woman's Journal* and *Weight Watchers* magazines. For many years she covered new output by singer/songwriters for *Top* magazine, which was distributed via Tower Records stores, and during this period interviewed the likes of Tori Amos, Tom Robinson and Joan Armatrading. As a freelancer for Independent Magazines she concentrated on celebrity interviews and film, theatre and restaurant reviews for magazines such as *Ms London, Girl About Town, LAM* and *Nine to Five*, and in her capacity as a critic she has appeared on both radio and television. She is currently the film reviewer for *Now* magazine and has written a number of titles for Trotman. When not attending film screenings she is active in the Critics' Circle and is the secretary for its film section.

Acknowledgements

Thank you to Andrew Bonnell, Jon Cox, Bill Vickers, Tamas Khan, Serene Tai Panayi, Marion Currell and Jacquie Moon for their contributions to this book.

Special thanks to People 1st for providing information on the hospitality industry, and to Birmingham College of Food, Tourism and Creative Studies for details of its prospectus.

Foreword

The catering and hospitality industry is diverse, providing meals for millions of people every day. Within this ever expanding market, food businesses are increasingly aware of the requirement for a well trained professional workforce.

Working within the catering industry is hard work but the rewards can be massive. You can be your own boss, work anywhere in the world and you'll be following a career in something that you really enjoy. All you need is enthusiasm and the right training to get you moving. City & Guilds can help with that, just like we've helped many top celebrity chefs before you…

Gary Rhodes, former City & Guilds trainee – now a celebrity chef and City & Guilds fellow
'I strongly believe my own City & Guilds qualification gave me a strong base to work from when aiming for my goals.'

As the leading awarding body within this field, City & Guilds has a long tradition of offering high-quality qualifications to the catering and hospitality industry. Many of our qualifications are still seen as the benchmark for chefs wishing to gain employment in the industry. Working closely with the sector skills council to ensure that the high standards are met, we have created a wide range of qualifications suitable for every level of learner. City & Guilds is delighted to be part of the Trotman *Real Life Guides* series to help raise your awareness of these vocational qualifications.

If a career in catering is for you, why not visit the City & Guilds website for more details: www.cityandguilds.com.

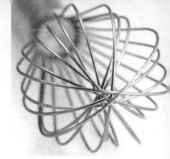

Introduction

Eating is one of the great pleasures in life – it's also a necessity. We all have to eat to survive, and yet how many of us, as we sit down in a restaurant to tuck into a delicious piping-hot pizza, or a fabulous five-course feast, ever think just how much effort and how many people it has taken to get that food to our mouths? The catering business is huge – in fact, the restaurant market alone is worth £17 billion and that's before you add in revenue from catering companies offering meals in canteens and at outdoor events to gastropubs serving delicious meals and companies making speciality ready meals for supermarkets. Walk down any busy high street and you will see just how large and varied it really is. You'll probably pass a fast food outlet such as McDonald's or Pizza Express; there may well be one of the pub chains that also serve food, such as the Slug and Lettuce; there might even be a restaurant that boasts Michelin stars or a Tesco Metro offering ready-made sandwiches prepared by an independent catering company. Yet, no matter how varied the quality and price of the food they offer, they have one thing in common: they all need staff.

The industry has become more sophisticated and professional in response to people demanding better levels of service, customer care and wider product ranges as they become more knowledgeable about food and drink.

If you are considering a career in catering, you are doing so at a very exciting time. Never before has there been so much scope for getting on in the industry – mainly because Britain has never before seen so many new food outlets opening. According to

People 1st, the Sector Skills Council for the hospitality, leisure, travel and tourism industries, in 1990 less than 25 per cent of the total food expenditure in this country was on eating out. By 2006 that figure had risen to 37 per cent and it is predicted to rise again to the current US level of 50 per cent by 2025. There are now more than 106,500 restaurants across Britain. This is due to a number of factors, but mainly to social change. With changes in society come changes in our eating patterns. At one time, eating out was considered a great luxury and only for special occasions such as birthdays and anniversaries. Families tended to eat at home, with mum doing the cooking. But with more women going out to work, longer working hours for everyone, more young people leaving the family residence to set up home alone, and the rise in the fast food market, eating out has become an everyday occurrence.

Out-of-home activities are growing more dynamically than ever before, so the demands for every type of leisure, entertainment, eating and drinking experience are ever increasing.

Also, trends and fads in eating change. The rise of the celebrity chef and TV programmes such as *Hell's Kitchen* and *Jamie's School Dinners* have led to Britain becoming a nation of 'foodies'. In the spring of 2007 there were no less than 16 food-related programmes on terrestrial TV in one week including *Neneh and Andi – Dishing It Up*, *Ready, Steady, Cook*, *Gordon Ramsey's F Word*, and *Great British Menu*. Also, the rise in the organic market and government initiatives to get us eating more healthily, such as its food traffic lights system, mean we are more aware than ever before of what it is we are eating and what actually goes into our food.

Bill Vickers is the Marketing and Food Service Manager for the Compass Group, the world's largest and most successful contract food service company with brands that include Burger King, Roux Fine Dining and Delice de France, and he is well aware of how fast the market has changed. 'Compass has grown from sales of £450 million a year and 8,000 employees to more than £11 billion and 400,000 employees in over 40,000 operating units in 13 years,' he says. 'We produce 25 million meals a day and have only scratched the surface of what potentially can be done during the next decade and we are continually exploring opportunities in our existing avenues of business, while also creating new ones. Out-of-home activities are growing more dynamically than ever before, so the demands for every type of leisure, entertainment, eating and drinking experience are ever increasing. It's not the conventional venues or experiences either: customers want excitement for all the senses. This means more fun and excitement for the people engaged in delivering the service.'

At one time, many people had a poor opinion of a career in catering – many jobs were quite badly paid and catering positions were seen as 'lowly' – but that has changed. Bill Vickers explains: 'The industry has become more sophisticated and professional in response to people demanding better levels of service, customer care and wider product ranges as they become more knowledgeable about food and drink. This drives quality standards up and forces us to understand more about consumer needs and wants.'

At present nearly 1.5 million people around Britain work in the catering industry in over 130,000 enterprises. Yet even with all these people there are 30,000 vacancies annually for chefs in Britain and this is set to rise dramatically as we count down to the Olympics in 2012 where thousands more catering staff will be needed to feed and water the competitors, their training teams and all the spectators pouring into the country.

Catering staff don't just work in restaurants. They also work in less obvious surroundings. Patients in hospitals need to eat. So too do prisoners, schoolchildren and hotel guests. Someone has to prepare and cook their food, but opportunities in catering do not end at the kitchen doors. There are other areas of the catering industry to consider, such as waiting staff, bar staff, wine waiters (sommeliers), maître d's, and managers (there are currently 145,447 restaurant and catering managers in the UK). This is why catering offers such an exciting career choice for people who are considering their professional futures. The most ambitious may be aiming to follow in Jamie Oliver's footsteps and end up with their own TV shows and book contracts; others may simply want to cook quality food for their local community. Whatever your ambitions, if you are interested in working in a challenging and expanding market where you get the chance to meet new people and discover new tastes, methods and business practices, then a job in catering may well be just your cup of tea.

This book aims to help you discover whether you are suited for a career in the catering industry. It will help you pinpoint the mental, physical and social skills and strengths you need to get on. It will show you the great range of jobs available in the market, including some you may not have considered or known about before. It will give you practical advice on what qualifications you need and explain the many different options for training. Finally, it will point you in the direction of the main industry and government boards and bodies responsible for that training. In catering, the world really can be your oyster, or crab or even lobster. It's up to you to make the choice.

ANDREW BONNELL

Success story

MANAGING DIRECTOR, LONDON BRASSERIES GROUP

After getting a degree in English, Andrew joined Allied Breweries in 1985 as an Area Manager and stayed with the company until the early '90s when he joined the Pitcher & Piano pub group. At the time it only had three bars and was operating at a loss, but over a five-year period Andrew helped transform it into a £30 million business.

In 1999 he left in order to lead the buy-in of the Toutsles chain of restaurants and took that from five restaurants to 35, with each branch turning over £10,000 a week and making about £100,000 profit a year per restaurant. The business was sold in 2005 for £35 million.

In the interim Andrew became the principal shareholder in the Brackenbury Restaurant Group in 2003 and in 2006 he set up London Brasseries to develop a nationwide group of upscale restaurants providing fresh, high quality and interesting food in a local setting. He currently has restaurants in Bluewater Shopping Centre, Wandsworth, Portsmouth, Manchester and Cardinal Place in Westminster.

I want to employ people who understand customers ... be that from a barman making someone feel really special to a chef making fabulous food.

'I'm not from a hospitality-trained background but what I do is to look at things from the customers' perspective. My job in this business is to say: how does what we are offering match with the customers' desires? So, I get very good chefs and very good barmen to deliver what the customer wants. I know what is good and what isn't and I look at it from a very personal point of view.

'I want to employ people who understand customers. What I don't want are chefs who think the be-all and end-all is a piece of art on a plate. My chefs should want customers to walk out of here with a full tummy and feeling good, be that from a barman making someone feel really special to a chef making fabulous food. You can train professionalism and teach your staff how to do the job, but you cannot teach people how to want to serve – they either do or they don't.

'The people who do invest in training do reap the benefits. At Pitcher & Piano we invented something called The Academy which was a training course for would-be managers. We discovered that in order to get on people had to be bright but more importantly, they had to be very empathetic. That's right at the heart of people in the service industry. They seek to make others feel good about themselves. They also need to be very hard-working, diligent and conscientious. They also have to be tolerant and have a desire to achieve within a value-oriented framework. What I look for is people with very sound verbal reasoning skills – you have got to be able to communicate – and good problem solving skills. I'm not overly bothered by mathematical skills. They have to be highly motivated and have enthusiasm and, over and above anything else, they have to want to do it.

'I'm very keen on my staff advancing and gaining promotion. We encourage the pursuit of vocational qualifications and pay our staff very well because they work long hours and they deserve it. I want my staff to feel their jobs are valuable and important and are recognised as being such.

'I think the future of the industry is very rosy because my view is that eating out is now firmly established as part of the leisure process and therefore people will continue to do it, even in a recession. I love what I do. I never wake up with that I-hate-Monday-morning feeling. It's full-on and it's brilliant.'

What's the story?

So you've decided you want to enter the busy and exciting world of catering. But do you really know what that world is all about? It is about the chefs and waiters at the local hotel, the waitresses at the Harvester Inn, and the lady preparing all those delicious soups and sandwiches at the deli in the high street. But it is also about the people preparing the food served at your school and the manager at the staff canteen of the large company down the road. Then there are the outside caterers who prepare all the meals for the actors and technicians on location for films and television, and at large private functions such as marquee weddings, or sporting events such as Royal Ascot. The catering world is actually made up of five sectors:

- hotels
- restaurants
- pubs
- contract catering
- hospitality services.

Of these, it is the restaurant sector that is the largest employer, yet that does not mean working in a restaurant will necessarily mean being employed by a big company. Three-quarters of catering establishments employ fewer than four people. We will be looking at the different aspects of working in each sector and how you can gain entry to them in more detail later in the book, but here you can see the nature of the jobs available in catering.

IN THE KITCHEN

The kitchen is the heart and soul of any catering establishment. It can be a small, compact unit only big enough for two people to work in, or a huge, state-of-the-art workplace fitted with numerous stoves and hobs, and alive with energy and people. Catering is an industry in which employees usually start at the bottom and then, as they gain more experience, work up through the ranks. Starting at the basic level in a kitchen is the kitchen assistant.

Kitchen assistant

The kitchen assistant helps to keep the kitchens clean and hygienic, receives deliveries and keeps the stores in order. He or she may also be involved in food preparation.

Catering assistant

This is the name given to people who carry out a kitchen assistant's duties but work in the institutional (hospitals, prisons) or contract catering sections (works canteen, motorway service station) rather than in hotels or restaurants. Their involvement in food preparation will be more detailed and they may well find themselves making salads, desserts and sandwiches.

In traditionally run kitchens in restaurants and hotels you then progress to the following levels.

Trainee chef

The most junior member of a chef's team, the trainee chef gains invaluable experience in all areas of the kitchen. Trainees will be supervised as they learn the basics of cookery, food quality, safety and hygiene, and once judged to be competent (usually after three years) they move up to the position of:

Commis chef

At commis level, a chef is still very much in training, being supervised while he or she cooks the less elaborate dishes on the menu. It is usually three years before the commis chef will be judged able to move on to the next level:

Chef de partie
The partie system is the traditional way in which areas of responsibility are broken down in a kitchen: each chef is responsible for a different section (partie) of the meal. For instance a chef patissier is responsible for desserts, while a chef poissonier deals with fish dishes. The chef de partie will be expected to master each of the different areas and will help to plan menus before becoming a:

Sous chef
With so much experience, the sous chef is responsible not only for food preparation but also for supervising junior staff and taking a certain degree of managerial control over the kitchen, such as ordering in the supplies. He or she acts as deputy to the:

Head chef
The head chef is responsible for everything that goes on in the kitchen and must liaise closely with the manager of the hotel or restaurant in which they work. They are in charge of their staff, plan the menus and in most establishments will be in charge of the kitchen finances, buying in the raw produce and negotiating with suppliers. Most head chefs have at least 10 years' experience in the industry, but since trainees start so young, you can still make it to head chef before you are 30 years old.

Cook
A cook will have similar duties and responsibilities to a chef, but the level of cooking tends to be more basic. A cook usually works in a contract kitchen such as in a school, a business canteen or a hospital, rather than a hotel or restaurant.

Contract catering

Contract catering is when an outside firm is contracted or employed to provide the cooking and meals for another company. For example, many staff canteens in offices and factories are supplied by outside catering companies; so too are school meals and the meals in hospitals. LSG Sky Chefs provide in-flight meals for airline passengers, and By Word Of Mouth is an independent catering company providing the food, waiting staff and even the crockery and cutlery for private parties and functions (see Case Study 2 with Colin Gray on page 39). The jobs within contract catering include cooks of all abilities (you could be preparing sandwiches or elaborate banquets), waiting staff (including counter serving staff) and those in management positions.

Fast food cooks/service assistants

This is a rapidly growing section of the catering industry as consumers just love fast food. Fast food cooks prepare foods such as burgers, fried chicken and pizzas in establishments that may have a sit-down area but where a large proportion of their business is in the takeaway market (examples being Burger King, KFC and Pizza Hut). Fast food service assistants take people's orders and input them into computerised systems before handing over the ordered items to customers. Many fast food chains now have their own, well-established training schemes and there are opportunities to be promoted all the way up to management level.

FRONT OF HOUSE

Front of house is where the waiters/waitresses and managers meet, greet and serve food to the public. Here again, people tend to work up through the ranks – even the managers, who need to have intimate knowledge of all aspects of their operation.

Waiter/waitress

Waiters have a vital role to play in catering: they act as the line of communication between the kitchen and front of house. When they take orders from the public it is essential they are accurate, otherwise things can go badly wrong and tempers can get frayed. A waiter must be efficient, but also sociable and friendly. Duties involve setting tables, taking orders, delivering food from the kitchen, clearing tables and delivering the bill.

Sommeliers (wine waiters)

The sommelier is not just a bottle opener and pourer; he or she must be really knowledgeable about the wines served in their particular establishment. They must be able to recommend wines to go with certain foods, serve the wine and, in some cases, also look after the wine cellar and do the ordering.

Head waiter

Like the head chef, the head waiter is responsible for the staff under him or her. A head waiter must ensure everything in the restaurant is running smoothly and must sort out problems if they arise. The head waiter must have a close relationship with the restaurant manager as they will co-ordinate staff and service.

Restaurant manager

Although restaurant managers rarely serve the food, they often come up through the ranks and so have an intimate knowledge of the duties of their staff. They are responsible for the training and organisation of the waiting staff. They often oversee bookings and make sure things are running smoothly front of house. They must also liaise with the head chef to make sure customers receive their orders efficiently.

IN-BETWEEN

With the rise of the fast food market, there are also now many jobs that cross the boundaries between the kitchen and front of house. Where restaurants have food counters, for example in canteens, delicatessens and motorway service stations, the staff may be asked not only to prepare the food, but also to keep the counter well stocked and to serve the public.

Not all kitchens or restaurants are run in the same way. Often, the breakdown of a person's duties will depend on the number of staff available. In a small country gastropub, the owner may well be doing the cooking with the help of just one kitchen assistant, and the bar staff may serve food as well as drinks. But what every catering outlet needs is well-trained, disciplined staff who know what they are doing. This is why vocational courses are so well established in the catering world and why so many large companies such as Travel Inn, Harvester and All Bar One offer comprehensive training programmes that lead to properly recognised qualifications. It makes sense for them, as they can recruit through their own ranks, and it makes sense for you because you can progress quickly and not get stuck in an entry-level job. In the Training chapter (page 41) we will explore in greater detail what types of training are on offer. But before you get into the details of training you need to know if you have the qualities necessary to make it in this industry. The next chapter will help you judge if you have what it takes.

JACQUIE MOON

Case study 1

THE TRAINEE

A single parent with two children, Jacquie Moon returned to catering after a stint working in childcare. After answering an advertisement in the London Evening Standard, *33-year-old Jacquie got a job working as a waitress for Carluccio's Ltd.*

There are now 30 branches of Carluccio's Caffès and Jacquie worked in many London branches, quickly rising to the position of Supervisor. From here she went on to Carluccio's internally run management training programme, specially designed for staff members. Highly regarded by the industry (Carluccio's has gained Investors in People status), the programme includes training in every department, so Jacquie has prepared food in the restaurant, served in the bar and delicatessen, and shadowed management shifts. The amount of time the course takes varies from person to person, depending on their skills and abilities, and once fully trained Jacquie will be able to step into the shoes of anyone working at Carluccio's, from a kitchen porter up to the assistant manager.

'Catering is probably the worst job in the world to do if you have commitments of any description, even down to having a

This job suits people who don't want to go into an office and see the same faces every day. If you want variety and are lively then this will suit you.

relationship or having children. A lot of the time you are doing shift work and that's really demanding so you have to enjoy it, otherwise it creates a big hole in your life. Sometimes I have to be up at five in the morning and Carluccio's Caffès are open seven days a week so you have to work weekends as well.

'Physically the job is very demanding. You are on your feet throughout the day and it is not always possible to take regular breaks so you have to be a really motivated, energetic person who is prepared to work very hard. I do like being busy though; I could not be confined to a desk. I think this job suits people who

There is a lot of opportunity out there for people. The more hands-on experience you have to offer then the further you will go. You really have to take the bull by the horns and be interested. If you have been well trained and have the knowledge on board then you can really go out and sell yourself.

don't want to go into an office and see the same faces every day. If you want variety and are lively then this will suit you. You also have to like being confronted with problems because when you have 20 people at the front door waiting to be seated, sorted out and back to work by a certain time you can't panic. You have to be organised and be able to think on your feet.

'I love talking to people and love meeting new people. I'm very sociable but you have to accept that your customers are the public and there's a boundary there that you don't cross. You need to be quite thick-skinned because if problems do occur it can get rather heated. My advice is don't take it personally! Having said that, I do like it when I look around and see customers enjoying themselves and know that I am a part of that and am contributing to that.

'Business is booming and I can't see that tailing off. Carluccio's will be opening more branches in the next year or two. There is a lot of opportunity out there for people. The more hands-on experience you have to offer then the further you will go. You really have to take the bull by the horns and be interested. If you have been well trained and have the knowledge on board then you can really go out and sell yourself. In fact, the catering industry is now becoming very competitive. With more well-trained people coming through, companies can pick the best of the crop. My advice to those who really want to make it in this industry is don't go in and just be a waitress or say to yourself "I want to be a manager"; get as much experience in all areas as you can because if you are thrown into a difficult situation and show you can deal with it then you've got one over all the other candidates.

'At the moment I am learning so much that's enough for me. But I would love to have a place of my own. I think that is the goal for a lot of people who work in the industry and is the reward for all the hard, unglamorous work you have to do. A place of your own means you aren't answerable to anyone but yourself and you make the rules and things have to be done your way. A place of your own must be very rewarding.'

4

Tools of the trade

Food, glorious food – even the thought of plates piled high with fabulous dishes from around the world is enough to make many people's mouths water and for some it becomes a passion so serious they end up employed in the food industry. Talking to people who work in catering it soon becomes obvious just how much they love their jobs, but they are under no illusions about what hard work it can be. In this industry, if you are willing to put the hours in and do the hard graft you can move up the employment ladder very quickly, but you really do need to be hungry for it. Being ambitious is just one quality that will help you get on, but there are other qualities, talents and strengths that will help you to progress. Below we list the most important. Think of them as your tools, giving you that added extra on your way to success.

Many jobs in catering are physically demanding, so it is no wonder that so many people employed by restaurants and pubs are young (over a third of restaurant staff are under 20 years old). You have to be **physically fit** to cope with the work. Chefs and front of house personnel are constantly on their feet, bustling about, especially during the extra-busy breakfast, lunch and dinner periods, so you need to have stamina.

The nature of the industry also means that catering staff often work shifts, so you will have to be able to deal with the physical demands of **getting up extremely early** and of **working well into the night**. For those working in kitchens the physical demands are increased by the fact they operate in very high temperatures, with ovens and hot plates constantly on the go, so the old saying 'if you can't stand the heat get out of the kitchen' is absolutely true. Physically, it also helps to be naturally **dextrous**: chefs are constantly chopping and cutting with extremely sharp knives at breakneck speed, so being clumsy can affect your ability to do the job. The same is also true for waiting staff who have to juggle loaded plates and glasses while navigating their way around tables and customers.

Mental agility and **enthusiasm** are just as important as physical agility. Be eager, ask questions, look interested and take a positive attitude towards criticism. People who have more experience than you can teach you so much. Remember, working in catering is not a solitary occupation: people work in teams both in the kitchen and front of house. If you can think on your feet, really listen to other people's advice and take the initiative when you have to, other people in your team will know they can depend on you.

Catering is a people-oriented industry, so you need to be **lively** and **sociable** in order to get on. Good **communication skills**, an outgoing personality and an ability to remain even-tempered when under heavy pressure are all qualities both kitchen and front-of-house staff should cultivate. Chefs do not work in isolation; they are surrounded by their sous chefs, porters and waiting staff, and must be able to issue clear, precise orders to them all. They also have to deal with their suppliers and managers and explain their needs clearly and concisely. Receptionists, maître d's and waiting staff have to communicate not only with the kitchen staff but also, more importantly, with customers, who expect a high level of courtesy and service, so being a people person will really help you to get on. No one wants to go out to enjoy a lovely meal only for the occasion to be marred by a surly and sour-faced waiter. You really have to enjoy being in a social environment, even when you are working while everyone else is having a good time. You may be coming to the end of your shift, with tired and aching feet, but you need to keep a smile on your face.

Sometimes it is not so easy to smile when problems occur, but **problem-solving** is a key skill to have. This is because there are endless opportunities for problems to arise. A supplier may let a chef down at the last moment and an alternative must be found quickly; a mix-up with an order can lead to a dissatisfied customer; when three members of staff fall sick on the same day the manager must rearrange shifts in order for a full team to be on hand. Using your common sense and organisational skills to solve these problems practically and with as little fuss as possible increases your value as an employee.

Possessing a **good sense of humour** will definitely help when you hit problems. The people who rise the quickest in this industry are those who can carry on smiling while their establishment seems to have been hit by a tornado. Even if World War III erupts behind the kitchen doors, if you can keep your customers happy and satisfied then you've got what it takes to succeed.

Hygiene is of the utmost importance when you are working with food, especially when you are catering for large numbers of people. Employers will be more inclined to take on staff with **good personal hygiene**. This is not only true of those working in the kitchen, but also of those members of staff who have general contact with the public. Washing regularly and having clean hair and, especially, hands and fingernails (which should be kept trimmed short), indicates that not only do you care about your appearance, you also care about cleanliness.

The world of catering is a fluid and quickly changing environment where fads and trends can come and go almost overnight. A decade ago Thai food and restaurants were almost unknown in Britain, while ingredients such as lemongrass and lime leaves were unheard of. Now you can even find them on the shelves of your local supermarket. These changes in food fashions make a career in catering very exciting, but also mean you have to keep your eye on the ball in order to keep up with them. So being **open to new ideas**, being aware of what is going on and sustaining your interest are all vital whether you want to be a world-class chef or manage your own bar.

While these qualities and skills will help you to get on, there are also weaknesses and physical conditions that could hold you back. There are also downsides to working in the business that may make it unsuitable for you personally. You should take the following into consideration before embarking on a training course in catering, especially those based in the kitchen.

If you are prone to **fainting fits** or **dizzy spells in extreme heat** you may well find the intensely hot atmosphere in a busy kitchen is just too much for you to take. A trainee with the famous Roux brothers once described the physical conditions of cooking in their kitchen as being like a miner working on a coal face deep in a badly-ventilated mine shaft.

Those with serious **food allergies** are probably only too well aware of the dangers certain foods can pose. If you are a chef you constantly taste the food you are preparing – which could be life-threatening for those with a nut or fish allergy.

If your **religious beliefs** ban certain foods you will have to look long and hard at whether a job in catering is for you. For instance, both the Jewish and Muslim faiths forbid eating pork and bacon. Those following a strict vegetarian regime would not be able to handle the meat and fish found in so many dishes. Obviously, there are specialist restaurants that cater for different diets, but you need to ask yourself how severely this would restrict you from progressing in the industry.

All jobs in catering will involve being on your feet for most of your shift. This can cause health problems for some people and is one reason why so many waitresses wear support tights in order to guard against getting 'heavy legs' and varicose veins in later life. People who have a family or personal history of **back problems** should also be aware that being a chef or waiter involves a lot of bending, stooping, picking up and putting down that can lead to stiff shoulders and necks and more serious back conditions.

People in catering do not work regular nine-to-five hours – not even the management – so if you are looking for a job where you are free in the evenings, at weekends and over the big holiday periods (Christmas, Easter) this is definitely not the industry for you. Your shift pattern can also change seasonally, depending on the volume of customers at your establishment. A career in catering means working while your friends are out socialising and you will have to make alternative arrangements to see them. Of all the downsides to the industry, **unsocial hours** is the one most people cite as the biggest problem.

Although by law all kitchen and waiting staff should have regular breaks, the reality is that if the establishment they work in suddenly gets very busy it will be a question of 'all hands on deck'. Because of this, many catering staff find it **impossible to eat regularly**. Sometimes it will be a question of grabbing something and eating 'on the hoof' to keep going. Much of the time you will find yourself eating at the beginning or end of a shift, hours before or after everyone else has eaten. This can play havoc with blood sugar levels and if you are diabetic it is something you really have to keep your eye on.

Finally, don't panic! If your first instinct in a crisis is to run out of the door and never come back, or sit down, hyperventilate and burst into tears, then catering is really not for you. The preparation and serving of food often seems to hit one crisis after another so you have to learn to cope with the **pressure**. This is because problems have to be rectified immediately. If your restaurant is full of customers and your electricity goes off, you have to deal with it. If a catering company is organising a wedding in a marquee and there is a sudden thunderstorm, they can't send everyone to the pub instead. The ability to stay calm, think it through and sort it out proves you have what it takes to make it – and if you can do so and manage to retain your sense of humour, so much the better.

Now you should have a better idea of whether catering is the industry for you. If you are still keen on a job in this area, try this short quiz of general knowledge questions and scenarios that could crop up while working. Simply choose the answer you think is right or closest to what your own response would be. Seeing how you do will show you if your knowledge is as good as you think it is, but don't worry if you get some answers wrong: this is meant to be fun! Answers are at the end of the quiz.

1. Hollandaise, mint, and béarnaise are all types of:

    A. Herb?
    B. Sauce?
    C. Tea?

2. You are working in the kitchen and an order comes in for a steak done medium rare. The waitress comes back saying the customer says it is overcooked. Do you:

    A. Say it is perfectly cooked, turn it over and send it back out?
    B. Think the customer is always right so start again from scratch?
    C. Go into a huff and refuse to cook for the customer again?

3. Tapas is:

    A. A Greek dance?
    B. A type of sherry?
    C. Small dishes of olives, fish and meat served with drinks in Spain?

4. You are the most senior waitress working on your shift and in an unfortunate accident some olive oil has been spilled on a customer's suit jacket. He is demanding £200 compensation. Do you:

   A. Laugh and say he must be joking?
   B. Tell him he will have to write to head office to get it sorted out?
   C. Personally guarantee to take the jacket to a specialist dry cleaners, have it cleaned, and then send it back to him?

5. If a pasta dish is 'al dente' it means it is:

   A. Covered in a cream sauce?
   B. Slightly firm when you bite into it?
   C. Shaped like teeth?

6. It is the end of a lively evening and a large and raucous group is questioning some items on its bill. One man in particular is getting quite argumentative. Do you:

   A. Have a stand-up argument with him there and then?
   B. Take him to one side, sit him down with a coffee and reason with him slowly and surely?
   C. Take the contested items off the bill but ban the group from ever returning to the bar?

DID YOU KNOW?

The Patak's Indian food brand was set up in 1957 by LG Pathak. The company supplies over 75 per cent of Britain's Indian restaurants with chutneys and pickles.

7. Rump, T-bone and fillet are all types of:

   A. Mushroom?
   B. Pork?
   C. Steak?

8. You are the youngest chef in the kitchen and the head chef has just told you off in no uncertain terms about the quality of your vegetable preparation. Do you:

A. Argue with him, saying he is being unfair?
B. Take on board what he is saying and try to do better?
C. Just give up?

9. Would you ever use a blowtorch in the kitchen?

A. Yes, to do DIY with.
B. No, think of all that gas!
C. Yes, a specialist blowtorch can be used to caramelise sugar on desserts.

10. Balsamic, cider and malt are all:

A. Alcoholic drinks?
B. Types of vinegar?
C. Varieties of apple?

ANSWERS

1. B. Although mint is a herb and can be made into both a sauce and tea, hollandaise and béarnaise are sauces.

2. B. Of course, the customer isn't always right, but in this case you have to serve them a steak to their preferred taste. As you cannot un-cook the steak, the only solution is to cook a new steak for a shorter time.

3. C. Tapas are Spanish snacks served with drinks. The word actually means 'lid' and refers to the fact the snacks were traditionally served on small plates that were placed over the top of your glass like a lid.

4. C. This is an actual scenario. The waitress kept her cool and explained she could not just give the man £200, but would handle the situation personally by taking the jacket to the dry cleaners and ensuring its safe return to its owner. The result was one satisfied customer and a waitress headed for a management position.

5. B. The word dente means tooth in Italian. In Italy the preferred way to serve pasta is so that as you bite into it, it still feels slightly firm to the teeth.

6. B. No one in catering should have to take abuse from the public but inevitably, after a long evening of drinking, some people can become difficult to handle. This is where your people skills must come in. If you have tact and sensitivity, the situation can be defused. The worst thing to do is to lose your temper too. However, sometimes people just cannot be reasoned with and at this stage, as a final solution, you may have to ban or bar people.

7. C. These are three of the better-known cuts of beef. You can get pork fillets, but you can't get pork T-bone!

8. B. No one likes a smart alec, especially not in a busy kitchen where there is no time for the head chef to argue with you or keep correcting your mistakes. Remember, you are there to learn, so be eager to take any advice or tips you are given. The more enthusiastic you are, the quicker you will get on.

9. C. A specialist chef's blowtorch is just one of the many and varied kitchen tools and utensils now employed in the modern professional kitchen. You will need to learn how to recognise them and to use most of them.

10. B. Although cider is indeed an alcoholic drink as well as being a type of apple, all three are forms of vinegar used for anything from mixing with olive oil as a salad dressing (balsamic), to sprinkling on your chips (malt).

Having completed this section of the book you should have a better idea of whether you have the skills, basic knowledge and, most importantly, the desire to enter the world of catering. The FAQs chapter (page 33) looks at what the job can do for you in financial, personal and social terms.

5

A day in the life of an executive chef

Forty-four-year-old Tamas Khan joined the Jim Thompson's chain of oriental restaurants in 1997 as a wok chef. Since then, he has worked his way up to be Executive Chef for all 14 branches of Jim Thompson's and is responsible for creating a new range of healthy eating dishes recently introduced into the restaurants.

'I start at about ten o'clock every weekday when I go into the office I have above the Jim Thompson's in Putney. Here, I will go through all the mail and emails and do my planning for the week. I phone everybody including my suppliers and then I ring every branch of Jim Thompson's and talk to the managers and the head chefs and find out if they are having any problems.

Running 14 kitchens is not a one-man job and you need to get everybody behind you so I treat my staff like family and friends. They all have my mobile number and they can call me 24 hours a day.

'I don't get out of the office until about four o'clock in the afternoon and I choose one branch to go and visit. I'll get there at about five and could stay until ten, and in that time I will sit

down with the chef and have a chat about staff holidays or
shortages and we will also have a look at the kitchen to see if it
is being kept clean properly and to check the cleaning schedule
and log book. Running 14 kitchens is not a one-man job and you
need to get everybody behind you so I treat my staff like family

*I pop up to New Covent Garden Market around
midnight and spend a few hours talking to my
vegetable suppliers, checking the quality and the
prices, and seeing what is new.*

and friends. They all have my mobile number and they can call
me 24 hours a day. Sometimes they call me at two in the
morning because they need to place an order urgently and they
can't get through to the supplier by fax, so I have to ring the
supplier direct.

'At around eight in the evening, just before the restaurant I'm
visiting that day really starts to kick off, I go and talk to the
manager and to the floor staff and watch the food coming down
to see if it is up to standard. Once I've checked everything is all
right, I may go and visit another branch to see how busy they are
and pop in to check how the takeaway service is going. I'd say
65 per cent of my job is spent in the kitchens talking to people.

'Three times a month I meet up with suppliers. If I finish in a
restaurant at ten in the evening there is no point me going home
to bed, so I pop up to New Covent Garden Market around
midnight and spend a few hours talking to my vegetable
suppliers, checking the quality and the prices, and seeing what is
new. If I visit my meat supplier I like to ask where the meat is
from, how it is produced, what does it eat and how it is
slaughtered. I don't get home until the early hours and that is
when most of the restaurants close up. I still have to be available

as this is when the chefs go through their fridges and see what they need to re-order, so they may need to phone me.

'At the weekends I do something I love. Saturday night I'll walk into any of our branches, put a jacket on and go to work in the kitchen. It gives me more of an idea how my teams are actually working and lets me see if everyone is happy, and it also helps when I set about creating a new menu because I can check to see if new dishes are achievable in each different kitchen.

'I have a few hours off on a Sunday to do things like my laundry, but basically I work a seven-day week, and I love it!'

6

FAQs

By now, you will be aware that catering is a service industry in which you, the employee, offer a service to the wider public, whether they are students in a school canteen, tired travellers at a motorway service station or well-heeled diners in an expensive restaurant. Your care and attention enriches their lives, but how will working in this sector enrich yours? What will a job in catering bring to your life? Below is a list of common questions people joining the industry ask: the answers may help you to decide whether catering is really for you.

ONCE QUALIFIED, CAN I MOVE UP THE PROMOTION LADDER QUITE QUICKLY?

In catering you most certainly can. It is not uncommon to find people in their 20s already in supervisory and management positions. You can reach the position of head chef by your middle 20s and as the industry keeps expanding there are many opportunities for moving on or sideways. You can choose to specialise and diversify into other sectors such as sales and marketing, facilities management and finance and accounting.

WHAT WILL MY TYPICAL HOURS BE?

In this industry, there are no 'typical' hours. The very nature of the business means working flexible hours is the norm. Most chefs do work a basic 40-hour week, but this will usually be topped up with overtime. Many people in the industry do straight shifts or work split shifts (two separate periods of work during the course of a day). If you work in a restaurant or bar you will normally be working late hours as well, and you will probably be working weekends and public holidays. In contract catering, such as preparing school meals or running a works canteen, hours are likely to be more 'normal', and employees may work Monday to

Friday. Outside catering, such as for large sporting events or film location work, can be extremely varied, as such events can last for a single day, over a weekend, or for several weeks or months. As with many other service industries, Christmas and the New Year are the busiest times in catering, with special parties being organised, such as the now traditional office party, and more people treating themselves to a meal out, so you will probably be expected to work at this time.

WILL I GET TIME OFF FOR HOLIDAYS?

Yes, you will. Just don't expect it to be over Christmas! Some establishments do, in fact, close for the holiday period, but many others do not because they are so busy. However, after this hectic time, January is usually pretty quiet, which is why so many people in the catering trade take their holidays in January. The average holiday entitlement is around four weeks a year, but this will obviously depend on who you work for and in what capacity.

DID YOU KNOW?

Over 60 per cent of the catering workforce in Britain is female.

HOW MUCH CAN I EXPECT TO EARN?

Pay will depend on experience and expertise. Traditionally, trainee chefs and waiting staff were poorly paid for the hours they put into the job. However, as the profile of the industry has improved, so too have pay and conditions. As a commis (junior) chef you would be earning about £9,300, rising to between £11,400 and £16,500 for a chef de partie. Head chefs earn around £18,800 to £26,000, although many celebrity chefs (especially those with Michelin stars) earn a great deal more than that. For example, a head chef working at London Brasseries can expect to earn between £40,000 and £50,000. An executive chef working in a five star restaurant can earn between £80,000 and £120,000 depending on where the restaurant is situated. Skilled waiting staff earn between £10,000 and £20,000, depending on seniority, and they can supplement their incomes with tips. These days many establishments pool the tips and share them out between the whole staff. Because of the increased responsibilities of the position, at management level you could be earning anything between £40,000 and £60,000, (at London Brasseries, the top manager earns £75,000 basic and gets bonuses on top of that) but you will earn considerably more if you have responsibility for multi-sites or a whole group of premises.

Remember other benefits may include uniform, meals on duty, live-in accommodation and staff discounts.

Your care and attention enriches their lives, but how will working in this sector enrich yours?

WILL I BE ABLE TO USE MY SKILLS ABROAD?
Yes, you will. In fact huge numbers of British chefs and other catering staff are working all around the world as you read this. If you are employed in the kitchens of one of the large international hotel chains it is quite normal to spend time gaining experience in their hotels abroad. Many of Britain's best chefs have worked in such diverse places as Switzerland, Dubai, Hong Kong, France and America. As a UK citizen you have the right to work in any of the other European Union countries and there is a Young Workers' Exchange Programme for those aged between 18 and 28 years. This allows you to get some vocational training or work experience in another EU country for a period of time between three weeks and 16 months. Some people travel as part of their work, for example, preparing high-quality food on cruise liners, or for airlines or the railway. However, the places are limited and competition for them is high. If you think working abroad could be a career choice for you, you should consider doing foreign language GCSEs.

WHAT CAN I EXPECT TO GET OUT OF THE INDUSTRY PERSONALLY?

The chance to meet a broad range of people, great variety on the job and a real sense of achievement. With society's interest in food and all things foodie at an all-time high, there has never been a more exciting time to get into the catering industry. Every day there are new things to learn, new people to meet and new challenges to rise to. The one thing you won't be is bored, because this is a hectic and physically demanding career. Catering is a 'people' business and one of the most rewarding aspects of the job is the way you really do become part of a team. The other people you work with in your restaurant, bar or cafeteria are not only work colleagues: they are also the friends you will rely on when problems arise or you hit a particularly busy patch.

HOW WILL THE WIDER PUBLIC PERCEIVE ME?

As a professional doing them a service they are grateful for. Unfortunately, there will always be the occasional awkward customer, but for most people out to enjoy a lovely meal or a night on the town, the service you provide adds to their pleasure, and 'thank-yous' will far outweigh any complaints. At one time there was a social stigma about being 'in service', but this is no longer true. As the industry continues to expand, standards continue to rise, and people from all walks of life find themselves working in catering. It is now seen as a highly professional career.

EVENTUALLY, COULD I BE MY OWN BOSS?

You most certainly could. Many chefs and managers dream of eventually running their own establishment, maybe a sleepy country pub with great food, a small family-run hotel or a snazzy French restaurant in the centre of town. Owning your business is a huge responsibility, not least as far as money management is concerned (you will be responsible for everything from paying the wage bills to sorting out building costs and maintenance, and complying with legislation). Because of this, many people who want to own their own establishment decide to take further qualifications to increase their management and business skills.

7

COLIN GRAY

Case study 2

THE CATERER/PARTY ORGANISER

While he was still at school 26-year-old Colin was inspired when a person came into the classroom to talk about organising parties. He was captivated by all the talk of fireworks and food and so he decided to go to university to study event management and while there he worked as a waiter to get some experience.

After he graduated he first worked for a firm that only organised parties but did not do any catering; he soon realised it was the catering side of the job he liked the most. He left to join By Word Of Mouth, a London catering firm that designs events from private dinner parties to huge marquee parties (they cater at Royal Ascot every year) and parties held at exotic locations, such as the V&A and the Royal College of Art.

'My job is to meet with the clients and discuss what kind of party they want to hold and where they want to hold it. We talk about catering and if they don't have any idea what they want I give them ideas and show them photographs of other parties we have done so they can decide. We plan a menu and if there are quite a few people

I don't like being in an office and so I love the variety of what I do.

coming then we get the client back in to do a tasting of their proposed food with a few options so they can see what they prefer. I even talk to them about what kind of plates and glasses we are going to use and how the food is going to be presented. I have to be there on the night to make sure everything goes OK and that the staff are prepared. For a party of 100 you need at least 12 staff and I have to organise everyone from the chef – to make sure he knows the timetable – to the waiting staff.

'We've done parties where there were literally no catering facilities and we had to bring in tables, hot trays, cupboards, freezers and mobile ovens. Christmas is very busy for us but so too are June and July when we do a lot of garden parties, weddings and big sporting events such as Ascot, rugby and polo days. I don't like being in an office and so I love the variety of what I do and I get to see so many different places. For example, tomorrow night we are doing a big dinner at the London Aquarium and the night after that I'm doing a dinner at the Banqueting House. I also love working with such a close team and there is a lot of enthusiasm as everyone is working towards the same goal. I never sit back and think "oh, this job is boring!"

'During the summer the unsocial hours can get a bit much, especially when you find yourself still working at four in the morning. It can be quite stressful too, but if it has been a successful party the next day you do get a sense of achievement. You have to put in the extra hours and be prepared to work at weekends. Eventually I'd like to own my own company doing big events but at present I'm quite happy to stay here as it is a very competitive market and you need as much experience as you can possibly get. That's why I'd say if you want to make a success of catering you have to be passionate about it and be willing to start at the bottom and work your way up. Get some experience as a waiter or waitress and if you are willing to put the work in, you'll find it can be financially as well as personally rewarding.'

8

Training

The previous chapters should have given you a pretty good idea of whether a career in catering is for you or not. If you are certain that it is, the next thing you will have to consider is how you enter the industry. Because catering is such a dynamic and quickly expanding sector, there are now many ways in which you can get industry-recognised qualifications. These can make your progression through the ranks much easier and faster, and if you are serious about getting to the top of the profession they will definitely help you achieve your goal.

There are two main routes for getting into the industry and you should think about them both carefully before deciding which is right for you. Because so much of catering entails being hands-on, one of the best routes is to get a job or become a trainee. By doing so you learn your skills at the cutting edge, and you can gain qualifications at the same time. These could be National Vocational Qualifications or Scottish Vocational Qualifications (NVQs/SVQs), apprenticeships, or a part-time college course. Training programmes are usually run either by the employer alone, or by an organisation together with the employer, to provide both training on the job, which is supervised by a specialist, and training off the job at a college or training centre (either day or block release, or one or two evenings a week). The length of the programme varies from a few months to two years. Many of the larger employers, such as Carluccio's, Aramark, Pizza Express and Jury's Doyle Hotels, now run their own industry-recognised training programmes, giving you the chance to earn as you learn. The employer benefits because new staff are getting trained to their own specifications, making it much easier to recruit and promote from within the organisation. The benefits to you are that you are actually employed and earning wages, and you are gaining qualifications that will improve your career prospects and job security.

Alternatively, you could take a full-time college course. Most full-time courses last one or two years and consist of a number of modules that cover different aspects of the job. Most of these courses will lead to NVQs/SVQs from the most basic, level 1, up to level 4.

NVQs/SVQs have proved very popular within the catering industry but now City & Guilds has developed and introduced a new range of Professional Cookery Diplomas in order to bring some consistency to the standard of full-time college courses. The new awards will be delivered as Vocational Related Qualifications (VRQs) rather than NVQs which means students do all their coursework in a college and must complete all 12 mandatory units to gain their level 1 or level 2 certificates. The reason for this change is so that employers know that employees with the new diplomas all have the same level of skill and ability. The Professional Cookery Diplomas also give students who do not want to go straight into a working kitchen environment, which can prove stressful for some, the chance to learn a full set of skills in the classroom. The diplomas will complement the existing range of City & Guilds NVQs/SVQs and once students have completed the diploma course they can either progress into employment or go on to do NVQs to perfect their skills. It is hoped a level 3 diploma will be available countrywide by the end of 2007.

Some universities and colleges also offer degree courses in hospitality and leisure and related subjects. There are a number of private colleges that also offer courses in catering: however, these can be very expensive and if you do decide to attend one you must check that the qualifications they offer are recognised by the industry.

NVQ/SVQ

At present, these are the most popular industry-recognised qualifications, where you are assessed on a continuous basis and which are awarded at four different levels. How long it takes you to complete each level will depend on how quickly you complete each unit of work, but many colleges offer full-time courses that cover both NVQ level 1 and NVQ level 2 and which last one year.

- Level 1 is an introduction to the job and ensures you have the basic skills, including hygiene.
- Level 2 is for more skilled workers who already know the basics. With this level you can enter the catering industry in a junior position.
- Level 3 is for workers with greater responsibilities who can cook much more sophisticated dishes and who may well be supervising other staff. You should have NVQ level 3 if you want to apply for a chef's job.
- Level 4 is for those who wish to enter management or become a head chef.

VRQ PROFESSIONAL COOKERY DIPLOMAS

These new awards are taught in colleges and students must complete all 12 mandatory units to achieve level 1 or level 2.

- Level 1 provides a good foundation in cooking skills, knife skills, kitchen organisational skills and time management.
- Level 2 ensures that students will be able to prepare and cook a wide range of dishes. The course also includes investigative and theoretical units to provide a broad understanding of all aspects of kitchen operations.

APPRENTICESHIPS

There are two main levels to the Apprenticeship scheme.

- Foundation Apprenticeship (FA), or Skillseekers in Scotland. This is equivalent to NVQ or SVQ level 2 and because you are working at the same time as learning it usually takes about 18 months to complete.

● Advanced Apprenticeship (AA) is equivalent to NVQ level 3 and normally takes between two and two and a half years to complete.

Apprenticeships are really aimed at school leavers and young people between the ages of 16 and 24. You are eligible for funding only if you finish your Apprenticeship by the age of 25. There is also a Graduate Apprenticeship (GA). This is only available to people who have already graduated in a non-hospitality discipline and, like the other Apprenticeships, it combines work-based learning with higher education. A GA usually takes between 12 and 18 months to complete.

BTEC HNC/HND

Edexcel administers the Higher National Certificate (HNC) and Higher National Diploma (HND) awards. These qualifications tend to be for people who want to go into management or who want to enter catering at a higher level. For example, to take the HND Hospitality Business Management programme you need to have completed NVQ level 3.

The Further Information chapter gives details on who to contact for these courses.

NEW TRAINING INITIATIVES

14–19 Diplomas

Currently in development are these exciting new diplomas. The 14–19 Diplomas are being introduced to act as an alternative to GCSEs and A-levels. Some 14- to 19-year-olds do not want to follow the traditional academic route of GCSEs and A-levels, and these diplomas will offer a real alternative. They are designed to prepare students for work or for further study at university by combining practical, on-the-job learning with more traditional learning. The Hospitality and Catering Diploma will have three levels:

- level 1 is broadly equivalent to 4/5 GCSEs at grades D–G
- level 2 to 5/6 GCSEs at grades A–C
- level 3 is equivalent to 3 A-levels.

Students will be able to progress from one level to the next. Most candidates will go from level 1 to level 2 or level 2 to 3. It is hoped the 14–19 Diplomas in Hospitality and Catering will be available from 2009.

Young Apprenticeships

The Young Apprenticeship (YA) programme is a new route at Key Stage 4. The programme allows motivated and able pupils to study for vocational qualifications, not just in the classroom, but also in college with training providers and in the workplace. Pupils are based in school and follow the core National Curriculum subjects – but for two days a week (or equivalent) they also work towards nationally recognised vocational qualifications. There are a number of approved Young Apprenticeships available in the catering sector including Foundation Certificate in Food Hygiene, level 1, NVQ in Professional Cookery, level 2, and Intermediate Certificate in Food Safety. For more detailed information about Young Apprenticeships, go to www.vocationallearning.org.uk/youngapprenticeships.

Foundation degrees

For those people who are already working within the catering profession a foundation degree could be the way forward in their training and careers. Delivered in partnership with employers, they equip you with the relevant skills and experience to become supervisors, junior managers and owner-managers in small businesses and, as they can be studied for part-time, they allow you to get on with your job while you learn.

Each year around 2,000 graduates from hospitality, catering and related programmes enter the labour market. Approximately a third enter the hotel and restaurant trade. Many enter related sectors such as the licensed retailing and contract catering sectors.

Foundation degrees include the following: culinary arts, food safety and quality management, food and consumer management. For more information on foundation degrees go to www.foundationdegree.org.uk.

Although it is not essential to have paper qualifications to enter the industry, you will need some qualifications to get on to certain courses. For example, at Birmingham College of Food, Tourism and Creative Studies, there are no formal entry requirements to take NVQ level 1 Preparing and Serving Food. However, if you take NVQ level 3 Advanced Food Preparation and Cooking Certificate in Food Hygiene you will need to have NVQ level 2 Basic Food Preparation or an equivalent qualification. Whatever further education route you decide to take, it will be very useful to have GCSEs or Scottish Highers in English, Maths and a craft skill such as Home Economics. If you are thinking of working in the tourist area or abroad, modern languages are also helpful. Bear in mind that some college courses do require a minimum of four GCSE passes.

Getting good grades isn't the only thing you can do while still at school that will improve your chances of getting on in the industry. By far the best thing you can do – and all the professionals who have contributed to this book wholeheartedly agree – is to get some experience actually working in a catering environment. Arrange a Saturday job or holiday job with a hotel, restaurant, fast food outlet or private catering company. Even if your only duties are washing up and putting away you will get a taste of what really goes on and have the opportunity to watch what the trained members of staff actually do. This will really help you to decide if this is the career for you; and if you decide to take a vocational route, a prospective employer will be interested to see it included on your Personal Development Plan (PDP).

As anyone who ever turns on the TV these days knows, food and cooking are tremendously in vogue at present. There are numerous magazines and books out there offering both recipes and facts about food. Show your interest by either buying magazines or borrowing cookery books from the library and actually trying out the recipes at home. Keep up with the latest new ingredients and cooking techniques and by watching cookery shows on TV – it's surprising how much you can learn from the likes of Jamie Oliver, Gordon Ramsay and Nigella Lawson. Also read the local papers: they will have news stories on catering premises opening in your area and you will be able to find out if you can do work experience with them, or if they have any trainee places available, by contacting them direct or by talking to your careers teacher or advisor.

Springboard UK specifically promotes careers in hospitality, leisure and travel and it has a network of centres across the country where over 14,000 people a year get free advice. It publishes some great magazines and pamphlets packed with information, and has direct links to the industry as well as schools and colleges. Each year it runs a national cookery competition called Futurechef for 12- to 14-year-olds, as well as a week-long careers festival, all of which can help to make you more prepared for a career in the industry. Explore the website at www.springboard.org.uk.

There are so many different course options – from basic bakery to advanced cake decoration, from advanced food service to restaurant management – that you need to know what is available and what you will be able to apply for. Once again, your careers teacher should be able to advise you, or you can check the websites of the bodies that award vocational qualifications (listed in the Further Information chapter) to see what courses best suit your needs and abilities.

Opposite is an easy-to-follow guide summarising all the information contained in this chapter, from entry level right up to the most senior positions.

access to

CATERING

NO QUALIFICATIONS	ENTRY LEVEL QUALIFICATION
	FOUR GCSEs (A-D) grades 1-3 **GNVQ/GSNVQ** level 1 **14–19 Diploma** selection interview

ON THE JOB TRAINING

APPRENTICESHIP ✦ TRAINEE SCHEMES

ADVANCED MODERN APPRENTICESHIP (England) **SKILLSEEKERS** (Scotland) **YOUNG APPRENTICESHIP** (England) **MODERN APPRENTICESHIP** (NI) **MODERN APPRENTICESHIP** (Wales)	e.g. **INSTITUTE OF CATERING**

e.g.
FOOD SERVICE ASSISTANT
CHEF/COOK
COUNTER ASSISTANT
KITCHEN ASSISTANT

CREDITS/FURTHER LEARNING

ON THE JOB QUALIFICATIONS ✦ PROFESSIONAL BODIES

NVQ/SNVQ level 1 **DIPLOMA (VRQ)** **BTEC HNC/HND** Full-time/part-time/distance learning	e.g. **HTF** (Hospitality Training Foundation), **INCI** (Irish Hotel & Catering Institute)

CAREER OPPORTUNITIES

DEVELOPMENT OPTIONS

HIGHER EDUCATION ✦ MANAGEMENT ✦ FREELANCE

Well trained

The training you receive in catering will be dictated by what you actually want to do when you leave college or finish your apprenticeship. For example, a trainee baker will learn all about fermented goods (bread), while a trainee doing a course on food and drink service will learn all about carving, filleting and silver service skills. However, as so much of the catering industry is concentrated on what happens in the kitchen, let's take a look at some of the skills and disciplines you will learn there.

Health and safety
Any kitchen where food is prepared for public consumption has to maintain strict hygiene levels – no one wants to be responsible for an outbreak of salmonella. Chefs and trainees must always keep the kitchen spotless and make sure there are no accidents that could contaminate the food being produced. Because of this the trainee's duties include an awful lot of washing and cleaning. Work surfaces must be washed down and kept sterile, and pots and pans must be thoroughly cleaned, as must crockery, cutlery and glassware. You will learn how to handle and maintain knives safely and at what temperatures certain fresh goods must be stored. You will also learn about hygienic storage of any prepared goods to be used at a future date.

Vegetable preparation
One of the first things a trainee chef learns is different ways to prepare certain vegetables and fruits. You will find yourself slicing and dicing an awful lot of carrots, potatoes, cucumbers and more exotic items such as pineapples, mangoes and artichokes. Through practice, chefs learn to do this almost in their sleep and become exceptionally dextrous with their knives.

Fast food preparation
Many courses recognise that a large number of trainees will go into the fast food business, so training will include lessons on preparing food for frying, grilling, steaming and boiling.

Dressing plates

Although at this stage you may not be actually cooking complicated dishes, the head chef may ask you to dress the plates before they leave the kitchen by adding garnishes, or by assembling some of the ingredients on the plate.

As you progress further (normally to NVQ level 2) you will be learning new skills, such as:

● Preparing and cooking meat

You will have to learn all about boning, carving and recognising different cuts of meat, how to preserve them and how to cook them. You will also learn about the relevant sauces to go with each meat dish.

● Preparing and cooking fish

Most fish doesn't come into the restaurant ready prepared, so you will be taught to fillet, scale and clean a wide variety of different fish. You will also learn about different cooking techniques.

● Dealing with deliveries

At this stage you will need to know how to receive and handle food deliveries so they do not deteriorate in quality before being used.

Many courses will also teach you to cook basic pasta dishes, how to bake cakes and desserts, and also (in some cases) how to develop your knowledge of vegetarian food (a fast-growing sector of the market).

By the time you get to train for NVQ level 3 you will be involved in a much more sophisticated level of cooking, including shellfish, and marzipan, chocolate and pastry products, and you may also be taught about the use of wines and spirits.

9

Real lives

MARION CURRELL, EXECUTIVE CHEF

Marion started cooking for her family at the age of 8. Cookery was her favourite subject at school so she took a City & Guilds Food Preparation qualification, which she passed with credit. She currently works for the Ponti's group of cafés and restaurants which has nearly 40 outlets in and around London, employing 700 people and serving in excess of nine million customers a year.

What do you like most about what you do?

I love being constantly challenged and I enjoy developing new recipes. One day I am going to write my own cookery book – when I have more time!

What do you dislike the most?

Not having enough time! I don't get to spend as much time with my family as I would like.

What would be your best piece of advice for people coming into the industry?

Be prepared for hard work and long hours, listen and learn all you can because you can never know enough. You must pay attention to every detail and always do your best. There is no room for half efforts in this business. You must have a real passion for food, be a good team player and have good people skills.

SERENE TAI PANAYI, WAITRESS

Twenty-eight-year-old Serene works with her mother in their own small establishment called the Amazon Café, in Islington, north London. Founded in 1997, it can cater for 35 customers and serves full meals, sandwiches and homemade cakes. Serene was studying media studies before she decided to work at the café full time.

What do you like most about what you do?

I enjoy meeting many different people every day. They keep the work interesting. It is very gratifying when they clearly enjoy being there and eating our food. I very much enjoy the adrenaline of the fast pace and the people I work with.

What do you dislike the most?

It can be very tiring at times and occasionally you can come across some very rude customers. Also, I work weekends, which are very busy, but you do get used to that.

Would you like to gain professional qualifications?

I most certainly would. I have decided to study business management in the evenings. Once I have completed the business studies course, I will write up a business plan and then open my own bar or restaurant. I'd say to anyone coming into the industry study as much as you can first because you can then enter the profession at a higher level. However, my best piece of advice is to wear comfortable shoes!

10

Career opportunities

In the What's the Story? chapter, we looked at just some of the jobs open to people who enter the world of catering. You probably won't have a concrete plan of exactly where you want your career to go until you start training, but it is never too early to check out your options. For instance, you may begin by training in the kitchens only to discover you'd much rather be doing a job that brings you more into contact with the public. Alternatively, you may decide you are more interested in fine wines than food and decide to become a sommelier. Remember, the skills you learn as you train will stay with you for the rest of your life and will very much determine just how far you climb on the professional ladder. You may be quite content to reach the level of middle management, or your ambition could be to own and run a whole chain of themed bars. The Chief Executive of the Compass Group started in catering as a 16-year-old trainee chef, so just think how far you could go! The following diagram will give you a rough idea of what's actually out there for you and just how far you can go.

We have discussed most of these jobs already but there may be a few you don't recognise. A maître d'hôtel, or maître d', is a hotel or restaurant manager who greets customers or guests and ensures their visit or meal goes smoothly. The maître d' is very much the captain of the ship and is seen as the ambassador for his or her establishment.

Consultants tend to work for the big restaurant chains, but they can also be employed by smaller establishments. They give advice on all manner of details from how a restaurant should look (down to the shape of the plates and colour of the tablecloths), to what dishes will work. Many celebrity chefs, such as Gary Rhodes and Jamie Oliver, also act as consultants to big brand food producers and supermarket chains.

Private chefs are hired by individuals or big companies to cook exclusively for them. Many large country houses have their own private chefs, as do large companies where the chef cooks for the CEO or members of the board (especially if they do a lot of corporate entertaining). Other private chefs concentrate solely on cooking for private dinner parties.

In fact, a job in catering is a bit like food itself: it can be a simple meal of just one dish or a blow-out feast of five courses. What you make of it will very much depend on how far you want to go, but there are thousands of different opportunities out there for you, each offering both personal and financial rewards.

This is an industry with real opportunities for advancement. As you go through the training and discover where your strengths lie you will be able to map out a future career path. The diagram below shows options that will open up to you once you have trained.

CAREER OPPORTUNITIES

BASIC TRAINING IN CATERING

WAITER/WAITRESS ♦ COUNTER STAFF ♦ KITCHEN ASSISTANT

MORE TRAINING / NVQ LEVEL 1&2

TRAINEE CHEF ♦ SOMMELIER
RESTAURANT RECEPTIONIST ♦ HEAD WAITER

MORE TRAINING / NVQ LEVEL 3&4

MAITRE D' HOTEL ♦ MANAGER ♦ CONSULTANT
SOUS CHEF ♦ HEAD CHEF/HEAD COOK

11

The last word

If you have made it this far through the book then you will have probably made up your mind whether a career in catering is for you. If you think it is, then you have made a good choice. As Bill Vickers of the Compass Group says, 'a job in catering is fun, demanding, satisfying, rewarding and privileged – we have the opportunity to experience and be involved in things most of the general public may only dream of!' It is a career path that can take you a long, long way. But, before you start contacting the relevant bodies about your training options, on the next page is a fun guide to see if you really have got what it takes to succeed in the catering sector.

Catering is a career that really does have an amazing future. The fastest growing areas at present are contract food service and budget hotel businesses, and other major growth areas include themed public outlets, fashionable eateries, healthcare (National Health hospitals, private hospitals, clinics and care homes), education, vending and casual dining. If you would like to work with people in a job that offers a wide variety and interesting experiences then this really is for you.

If you have made it this far through the book then you should know if **catering** really is the career for you. But, before contacting the professional bodies listed in the next chapter, here's a final, fun checklist to show if you have chosen wisely.

THE LAST WORD   ✔ TICK YES OR NO

DO YOU LIKE WORKING WITH YOUR HANDS?
☐ YES
☐ NO

DO YOU LIKE WORKING WITH PEOPLE?
☐ YES
☐ NO

DO YOU CONSIDER YOURSELF CREATIVE?
☐ YES
☐ NO

DO YOU WANT A JOB WHERE YOU WILL BE DOING SOMETHING DIFFERENT EVERY DAY?
☐ YES
☐ NO

ARE YOU SELF-MOTIVATED AND ABLE TO THINK ON YOUR FEET?
☐ YES
☐ NO

ARE YOU ABLE TO COMMUNICATE EFFECTIVELY WITH LOTS OF DIFFERENT PEOPLE?
☐ YES
☐ NO

ARE YOU A SELF STARTER, ABLE TO TAKE CONTROL AND RESPONSIBILITY?
☐ YES
☐ NO

If you answered 'YES' to all these questions then
CONGRATULATIONS! YOU'VE CHOSEN THE RIGHT CAREER!
If you answered 'NO' to any of these questions then this may not be the career for you.
However, there are still some options open to you,
for example, you could work as a waiter/waitress, bar person or at a food counter

12

Further information

Listed below are all the addresses, telephone numbers and websites of the major government and industry bodies responsible for training in catering. There is also a list of publications you will find useful for background information and news on the industry.

TRAINING AND ADVICE

City & Guilds

1 Giltspur Street
London EC1A 9DD
020 7294 2800
www.city-and-guilds.co.uk

City and Guilds is the leading provider of vocational qualifications in the United Kingdom. It offers six types of qualification including NVQ and SVQ, Apprenticeship, Key Skills, Progression Awards, Higher Level Qualifications, Senior Awards, and its own City and Guild qualifications. The website gives comprehensive information on what courses are available and also where you can train.

Connexions

www.connexions-direct.com

Connexions is aimed primarily at 13- to 19-year-olds, but is an excellent source of information for all ages. If you click on the Jobs4u section on the homepage you will find a huge career database including information on the catering sector.

Apprenticeships
Packs available from 0800 585505
www.apprenticeships.org.uk

If you are undertaking a vocational training course lasting up to two years (with one year's practical work experience if it is part of the course) you may be eligible for a Career Development Loan. These are available for full-time, part-time and distance learning courses and applicants can be employed, self-employed, or unemployed. The government pays interest on the loan for the length of the course and up to one month afterwards.

For Modern Apprenticeships in Scotland:
0845 8502 502
www.scottish-enterprise.com/modern-apprenticeships

For Modern Apprenticeships in Wales:
029 2090 6801
www.careers.wales.com

For Traineeships in Northern Ireland:
0800 100 900

Edexcel
One90 High Holborn
London WC1B 7BH
0870 240 9800
www.edexcel.org.uk

Edexcel is responsible for offering BTEC qualifications including BTEC First Diplomas, BTEC National Diplomas, and BTEC Higher Nationals (HNC and HND). It also offers NVQ qualifications. The website includes qualification 'quick links' and you can search by the qualification or the career you are interested in.

HOW DO I KNOW WHICH JOBS ARE RIGHT FOR ME?

No problem, you can log onto **cityandguilds.com/myperfectjob** and take 20 minutes to answer a range of online questions which looks at your interests, personality and lifestyle and suggests job areas which may suit you. Get all the information on job options, how to get started and where you can go to study.

cityandguilds.com/myperfectjob

Food and Drink Qualifications Council
6 Catherine Street
London WC2B 5JJ
020 7836 2460

Hospitality Awarding Body (HAB)
International House
High Street
London W5 5DB
020 8579 2400
www.hab.org.uk

HAB is the awarding body of the Hospitality Training Foundation, awarding both NVQs and VRQs in such subjects as conflict handling. There is a comprehensive list of awards on the website.

Irish Hotel and Catering Institute
www.ihci.ie

This is the professional body for managers in catering in Ireland.

New Deal
www.newdeal.co.uk

If you are an older individual looking to change careers and you have been unemployed for six months or more (or receiving Jobseeker's Allowance), you may be able to gain access to NVQ/SVQ courses through the New Deal Programme. People with disabilities, ex-offenders, and lone parents are eligible before reaching six months of unemployment. Check out the website for more information.

People 1st
2nd Floor, Armstrong House
38 Market Square
Uxbridge UB8 1LH
0870 060 2550
www.people1st.co.uk

The Sector Skills Council for the hospitality, leisure, travel and tourism industries. Its comprehensive website is packed with information about these industries and includes news bulletins and research papers, facts and figures, and new training initiatives.

Qualifications and Curriculum Authority (QCA)

83 Piccadilly
London W1J 8QA
020 7509 5555
www.qca.org.uk

In Scotland:

Scottish Qualifications Authority (SQA)

Optima Building
58 Robertson Street
Glasgow G2 8DQ
0845 279 1000
www.sqa.org.uk

These official awarding bodies will be able to tell you whether the course you choose leads to a nationally approved qualification such as NVQ or SVQ.

Springboard UK Ltd

3 Denmark Street
London WC2H 8LP
020 7497 8654
www.springboarduk.org.uk

Springboard was set up to promote careers in hospitality, tourism and leisure, and offers a specialist careers service giving free advice. Each year it organises a week-long Careers Festival, and a national cookery competition for 12- to 16-year olds entitled 'FutureChef'. It also offers work experience programmes and an interactive CD-ROM called Springteractive.

PUBLICATIONS

Caterer and Hotelkeeper
www.caterer.com

The main publication for the industry; it is packed full of features and also advertises up to 20,000 job vacancies at any one time. The website is an excellent resource.

Hotelier
www.hoteliermagazine.co.uk

Published six times a year: news and views on the hotel trade.

Catering in Scotland
www.cateringinscotland.com

This brilliant, bi-monthly publication has in-depth features, news and views on catering north of the border